RELIGIONS OF HUMANITY

Chelsea House Publishers
1974 Sproul Road, Suite 400
Broomall, PA 19008

The Chelsea House
world wide web address is
www.chelseahouse.com

English-language edition
© 2002 by Chelsea House
Publishers, a subsidiary
of Haights Cross
Communications
All rights reserved.

First Printing

1 3 5 7 9 6 4 2

Left: Face of a reclining Buddha. This monumental statue, which shows the smile of the Buddha, transmits a profound serenity. The statue is located in a magnificent sanctuary, surrounded by monasteries, in one of the most ancient cities of the kingdom of Siam, Nakhon Pathon (now Thailand).

Opposite: Children playing under the care of Tibetan monks in their place of exile in India, where the Dalai Lama and many Tibetans have found refuge.

Library of Congress Cataloging-in-
Publication Data Applied For:
ISBN: 0-7910-6626-6

© 2000 by
Editoriale Jaca Book spa, Milan
All rights reserved.
Originally published by
Editoriale Jaca Book, Milan, Italy

Design
Jaca Book

Original English text by
Julien Ries

JULIEN RIES

THE MANY FACES OF
BUDDHISM

CHELSEA HOUSE PUBLISHERS
PHILADELPHIA

CONTENTS

INTRODUCTION

More than 2,500 years ago, after a long and difficult search, Siddhartha Gautama suddenly discovered the solution to the problem of human suffering that had tormented his soul. After a night spent in meditation beneath a *pipal* tree, he achieved "the Awakening to Truth" (or "the Enlightenment") and thus obtained the supreme peace of the extinction of passions and the definitive liberation from suffering and from the cycle of rebirth.

Resuming his pilgrimages, the Buddha shared this wisdom with his fellow men, leading them on the path of liberation from suffering, and beginning his role as guide and physician to humanity. This work will seek to explain the fundamental elements of Buddhist wisdom — from the Buddha's concept of man and of the human condition in the cosmos to the role of human action charged with a karmic power (relative to the law of cause and effect found in actions); the idea of *nirvana*; the noble path of Awakening; and the three refuges: the Buddha, the Law, and the Community.

After 2,500 years, Buddhism continues to be the revered religion of much of humanity. Over the centuries, in its encounters with other cultures, Buddhism has undergone several changes, which have given it a historical complexity vital to our understanding of its various facets. At the beginning of the common era a new Buddhism of devotion arose from contact with Hinduism. Over these two millennia, the disciples of the Buddha have organized themselves in a number of schools and approaches, in regard to both meditation and devotion. The last chapters will provide a few ideas about this vast movement.

Opposite: An extraordinary image of the Buddha, a masterpiece of Indian art, found in one of the rupestral temples at Ajanta in India.

Right: A Tibetan refugee in India. The tragedy of the exile leads to the exercise of the fundamental attitude of Buddhism: compassion.

1
BUDDHISM TODAY

Six centuries before the birth of Christ, in the valley of the Ganges river, Gautama the Buddha started preaching his message based upon a faith in the human being and on his ability to find peace and happiness through good actions. This wisdom was accepted in India, China, Ceylon (Sri Lanka), Tibet, and in all the countries of the Far East.

Europeans encountered Buddhism in the course of the nineteenth century as a result of colonization, but they did not find it easy to understand. Some European colonists opposed it in the name of their religion, while others welcomed it with a romantic enthusiasm.

Today the situation is very different, with modern Buddhism seen as a universal message. In 1956, on the two-thousand-and-five-hundredth anniversary of the Buddha's birth, an international Buddhist congress tried to formulate precepts and indications favoring the expansion of the Buddhist message around the world, to start national and international associations, and to found a missionary Buddhist seminary in Bangalore in India. Since then Buddhist missionaries have been active all over the world.

Modern Buddhism is presented as an Awakening, so that man's behavior will lead him to the truth — and thus to liberation from fear, anguish, and suffering — starting him on the path to happiness. Surrounded in his existence by the flux of events, man resembles a wheel, an evolving creature, a nucleus of sentiments and will, a flame which feeds itself, an existence which depends on all that has gone before. Awakened to his duties, man must master himself, establish the balance between himself and the external world (other people and the environment), give direction to his sexuality with energy, and renounce the slavery of desire. The goal is to reach a state of peace (*nirvana*), which is a spiritual and physical balance characterized by goodwill and an attuning of oneself to others. Thus, for modern man, Buddhism offers itself as the path of Awakening to duty and progress attained through continuous personal effort, in a state of inner peace and benevolent compassion in social life, with a spiritual outlook at the world but without religious preoccupation. Conscious of the precariousness of the human condition, the Buddhist looks for his awakening, liberation from suffering, and inner enlightenment.

2. Solitude and repetitive physical labor in a great Chinese industrial plant.
3. Young Buddhist monks in Bangkok in Thailand. A master and his disciples dressed in sandals and traditional robes carry a camera and express serenity to passers-by.

1. War, which destroys both men and books, is shown in this well-known painting by Pablo Picasso, which is considered as a universal heritage. It is found in the chapel of War and Peace at Vallauris in France. The illustration shows a lithographic copy made after the completion of the chapel.

1

2
THE SPREAD OF BUDDHISM

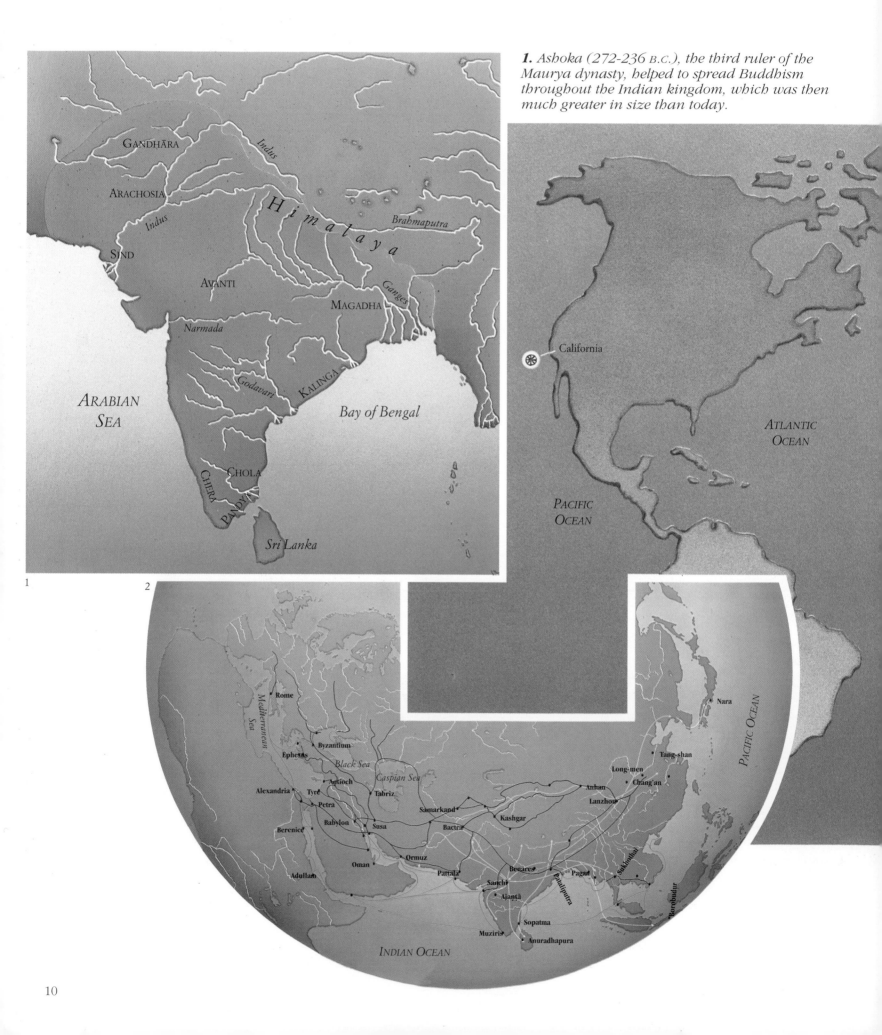

1. *Ashoka (272-236 B.C.), the third ruler of the Maurya dynasty, helped to spread Buddhism throughout the Indian kingdom, which was then much greater in size than today.*

GANDHĀRA

ARACHOSIA

Indus

SIND

Indus

H i m a l a y a

Brahmaputra

AVANTI

Narmada

MAGADHA

Ganges

Godavari

KALINGA

ARABIAN
SEA

CHERA CHOLA

PANDYA

Bay of Bengal

Sri Lanka

California

ATLANTIC
OCEAN

PACIFIC
OCEAN

1

2

Mediterranean Sea

Rome

Byzantium

Ephesus

Black Sea

Caspian Sea

Antioch

Alexandria Tyre

Tabriz

Petra

Samarkand

Kashgar

An'an

Long-men

Tang-shan

Chang'an

Lanzhou

Berenice

Babylon

Susa

Bactra

Adullam

Oman

Ormuz

Pattala

Benares

Pagan

Sukhothai

Sanchi

Pataliputra

Ajanta

Muziris

Sopatma

Anuradhapura

Borobudur

Nara

PACIFIC OCEAN

INDIAN OCEAN

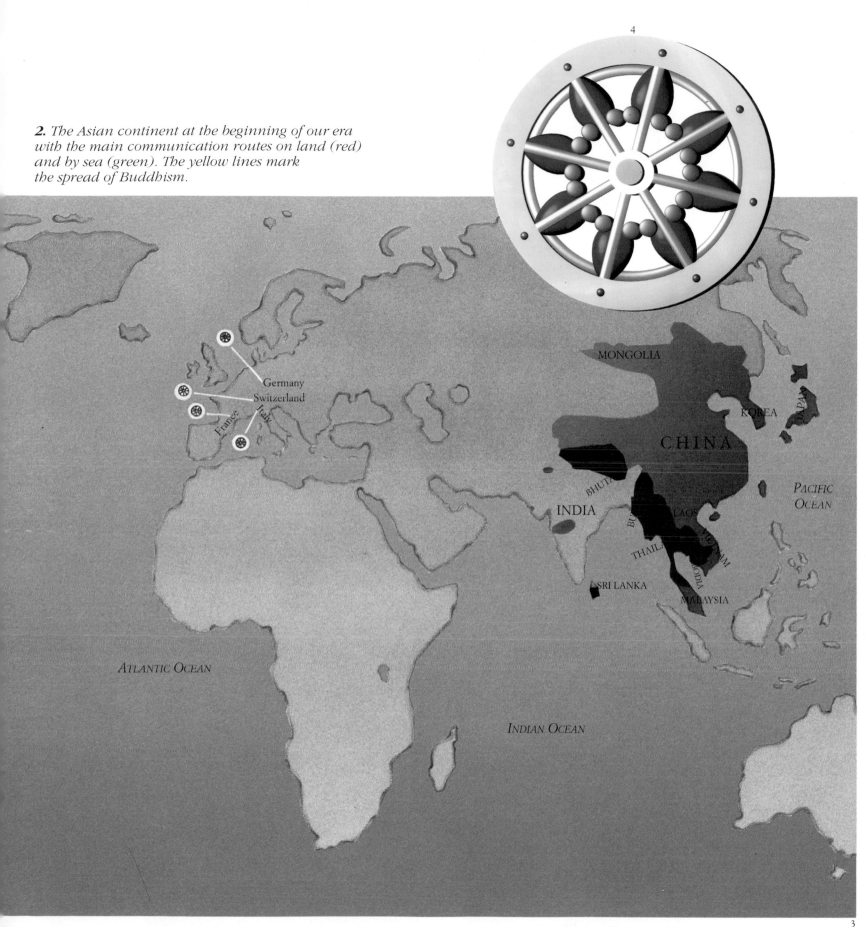

2. *The Asian continent at the beginning of our era with the main communication routes on land (red) and by sea (green). The yellow lines mark the spread of Buddhism.*

MONGOLIA

KOREA

JAPAN

CHINA

BHUTA

INDIA

LAOS

PACIFIC OCEAN

BU

THAIL

VIETNAM

SRI LANKA

ODIA

MALAYSIA

Germany

Switzerland

France

Italy

ATLANTIC OCEAN

INDIAN OCEAN

3. *The red parts on the map show the areas where Buddhism is today the majority religion; the light red shows where it is a minority; while the small wheels show particular presences in Europe and America. According to recent data, in TIBET, THAILAND, MYANMAR (BURMA) more than 85% of the population practice Buddhism; in KAMPUCHEA (CAMBODIA), LAOS, BHUTAN, and SRI LANKA between 70% and 85%; in JAPAN, MONGOLIA, TAIWAN,*

VIETNAM, and SINGAPORE between 40% and 55%; in SOUTH KOREA, HONG KONG, and MALAYSIA about 20%; and in CHINA about 6% (sources: Joanne O'Brien, Martin Palmer, Atlas des Religions dans le Monde, Myriad, London/Autrement, Paris 1994; Le Monde au Présent II, Encylopaedia Universalis, Paris 1994).

4. *As will be seen in Chapter 4, the wheel is an important Buddhist symbol.*

3
BUDDHA THE FOUNDER

Toward the middle of the sixth century B.C., Siddhartha Gautama was born to a prince of the noble clan of the Shakya at Kapilvastu, north of Benares, India. By the age of 29, he was married and the father of a son, but his life was disturbed by the tragic nature of the human condition. During this time, Gautama was struck by four encounters that had a profound effect on him. First, he met a decrepit old man, followed by a sick man bent over with pain, then a corpse carried to a traditional funeral pyre, and finally a serene and happy ascetic hermit. He started to wander in solitude, and one brightly moonlit night, as he sat looking eastward beneath a *pipal* tree,

he was suddenly enlightened and awakened to the Truth. He thus became the Buddha, also known as the Awakened One, Shakyamuni, the Sage of the Shakya.

After this profound spiritual experience, he again began to wander and in the Park of the Gazelles at Benares met five ascetic young men to whom he described the four noble truths he had discovered: 1) the truth about suffering: that indeed everything is suffering; 2) the truth about the origin of suffering, which is desire; 3) the truth about the surcease of suffering by suppressing desire; 4) the truth of the eightfold path leading to the end of suffering.

1. Below, left. The Buddha is shown within a circle of light, while the encounters that enlightened him to choose his path are shown around him. Prince Siddhartha Gautama first meets an old man, then a sick man, and then a dead man. These meetings show him the sufferings of man and the limits of life. His final meeting is with an ascetic hermit who shows him the path of spiritual seeking. Gautama puts on a monk's garb and starts his way toward Enlightenment. The larger picture shows the Buddha dressed up as a monk beneath a tree in garden near the modern city of Benares. This was the first public sermon of the Buddha.

The FIRST noble truth is something that the Buddha himself realized—that suffering, *duhkha*, is universal and can be found in birth, illness, old age, death, union with whatever one does not love, and separation from what one loves. Suffering is a state of agitation, unrest, conflict, and lack of harmony, but it does not impose itself as evidence.

The SECOND truth teaches that the origin of suffering is desire, *trishna*, which is the thirst for passions, a longing either for being or non-being, that chains each human to the eternal cycle of rebirth. The source of suffering can be found in the human conception of life: an illusory attachment to the self and to material things as if they were permanent. This ignorance leads man to egoistical actions from which he must purify himself through a number of rebirths.

2. A statue from the rupestral temple at Ajanta in India relates an edifying moral story. A little boy who has nothing to offer gives the Buddha a fistful of earth, showing that the intention behind a deed is more important than its results.

1

2

The THIRD truth, that of *nirvana*, leads to a state of repose, to the distancing of oneself from all things, to the extinction of desire, and to the cessation of all cravings. It opens the way to harmony and happiness. The attainment of *nirvana* involves several steps—beginning with the annulment of love, hate, and error in oneself, and ending with their extinction at the moment of death.

The FOURTH truth stipulates the eightfold path, the *marga*, which leads to *nirvana*. By following this path, one achieves morality through the commandments, the concentration or mental discipline needed to maintain a state of alertness, and finally, wisdom (*prajna*), which is the result of teaching, reflection, and contemplation.

13

MAN,
ACTION, REBIRTH,
NIRVANA

The cakra (the wheel) (1) is the symbol of impermanence. It rests on only one small point, which changes continuously. Thus man can never halt his life and guarantee some sort of arrival. Neither wealth, nor honors, nor successes can make life complete or stable. But every action of man is written in his karman and will have an effect. The slides show scenes of human activity at the end of the 20th century: a street in Peking in China

According to the Buddha, the human being is an accumulation of elements that are always in motion and that center around various experiences. Such experiences do not occur because of a self or a person, but constitute an ever-changing complex over time. These elements imply five fundamental aggregates (*skandha*), twelve bases, and twenty-two faculties of comprehension. Man performs actions. Each action is willed, that is, first thought and then carried out by means of the creative physical, vocal, and mental activities, which can be either good or evil. Each action carries in itself the effect of retribution, which man will inherit for his own happiness or sadness.

When the Buddha speaks of action, he uses the Hindu word *karman* as his keystone and emphasizes the inexorable link between actions and results. Each action produces the need for retribution, both in life and after death, since actions never perish even after millions of cosmic eras. The *karman* belongs strictly to the individual and is not transferable: it leaves its distinguishing mark on beings and is their property and their heritage. Because of the non-existence of the self,

(3), the harbor at Tokyo in Japan (4), a street in Bangkok in Thailand (5), the port of Bombay in India (6). Because of his bad or imperfect actions, man has to undergo various rebirths or achieve nirvana, the end of suffering and rebirth. The reclining Buddha shows the achievement of nirvana in the most perfect calmness. This statue (2) is to be found at Polonnaruwa in Sri Lanka.

the *karman* has its own efficiency. Therefore evil actions carry with them the necessity of rebirth in order to atone for them. The *karman* subjects the human being to the cycle of rebirth and of suffering (*samsara*). The collective force of actions (of the *karman*) creates, organizes, maintains, and conditions the entire universe, thus taking the place of god the creator, whom the Buddha never mentions.

Nirvana constitutes the end of suffering and rebirth, the reward of good actions. Being a state of freedom from the necessity of another rebirth, it resembles the extinguishing of a flame. It is the cessation of desire and as such can be reached in this life as the Buddha did in the moment of his Enlightenment. In short, it is the state of sanctity. The *nirvana* is, however, much more. It is light, joy, and fullness, perfect knowledge, unchangeable happiness, a perfect beatitude for the one who experiences it, that is the one who frees oneself from the conditioning of existence by death. This aspect, stated in Buddhist texts as 'the other bank, the island, the refuge, the retreat, the immortal, the wondrous state, the beatitude,' remains a mystery.

5
THE BUDDHIST COMMUNITY AND THE NOBLE PATH OF AWAKENING

As the one who started the walk (*marga*) that leads to liberation, the Buddha wanted to give his followers the means to reach their destination. In order to lead them toward *nirvana*, he founded a community of mendicant religious (*bhikshu*), who, wearing the yellow garb of Indian monks, follow the ten fundamental rules set out in 250 precepts, a number which is doubled for nuns. Each infraction of the rules carries with it a specific sanction. The monk is expected to live in poverty and is forbidden ten things: killing of living creatures, theft, incontinence, lying, fermented drinks, afternoon meals, dance, music and shows, floral wreaths and perfumes, sheets and luxury coverlets, and possession of gold and silver. Every 15 days, the monk must confess publicly any disobedience of the rules.

1

2

16

The monks, who must undergo a two-year novitiate and be ordained by a chapter of ten senior monks, become candidates for sanctity (*arhat*). Chaste and poor, and expected to meditate on the human condition, each monk must beg for his daily meal every morning. The monastic institution does not have a spiritual leader or hierarchy. There are only prerogatives regarding precedence, calculated according to the date of ordination. At any time, the monk can give up his duties and return to the secular world.

The Buddha (also called Shakyamuni or 'the Sage of the Shakya') completed his community known as *Samgha* with a brotherhood of 'lay persons' (*upasaka*), who were secondary but trustworthy members for whom generosity was the major reason for existence. It was the responsibility of these *upasaka* to build monasteries and obtain food and means of sustenance for monks and nuns. Immersed in the preoccupation of daily life, the lay person finds refuge in the Three Jewels: the Buddha, the Law (*Dharma*), and the *Samgha*, without hope of an immediate access to *nirvana*, but with the hope of better rebirths in the worlds of men and the gods. For lay people, generosity toward the religious is the best means to gain merits.

At Ajanta, in the Indian region of Maharashtra, 110 kilometers northeast of Aurangabad, there are 30 caves dug in the hard basalt rock, where a number of Buddhist monks settled in the second to first century B.C. and in the third to sixth centuries A.D. These painted caverns, originally meant to serve as shelter during the rainy seasons, offer a precious historic and archaeological record of the life of the *Samgha*.

3

4

1. A group of monks in the rupestral sanctuary at Yungang in China. Note the gigantic statue of the Buddha, which dates back to the end of the fifth century A.D.
2. 'Vihara,' a Buddhist two-storied rupestral monastery, at Ajanta, in India.
3. A statue of the meditating Buddha in the great Buddhist complex at Borobudur on the island of Java in Indonesia. This statue, a

symbol for monks, with the woods and the mountains in the background, expresses the conciliation with nature.
4. Monks playing musical instruments in the Tibetan monastery in Kampagar in northern India. Drums are a fundamental element for the rites and dances of Tibetan Buddhism.

FROM THE BUDDHISM OF THE *SHRAVAKA* TO *MAHAYANA*

During the first five centuries, all the disciples of Shakyamuni remained faithful to his teachings. Known as *shravaka*, listeners, they had collected three baskets (*pitaka*) of writings that date back to the Master himself: discipline (*vinaya*), the sermons (*sutra*), and the doctrine (*abhidharma*). The conversion of Emperor Ashoka (272-236 B.C.) and his missionary zeal gave the decisive impulse for the spread of Buddhism throughout India and in Ceylon from 250 B.C. These are the centuries of *Hinayana* (or Small Vehicle) – a Buddhism essentially for monks – which saw the foundation of various schools and sects, resulting in the convening of a number of councils. Numerous documents show the great influence of the monasteries on Indian culture.

The lay people still turned toward the *jataka*, narratives of the previous lifes of the Buddha. In particular, they admired his great shows of generosity, patience, and energy. The supreme and perfect Awakening attracted them more than did the sanctity of the monks. Concerned about their own spiritual, mythological, and religious needs, they created the figure of the *bodhisattva*, a personage who is no more a guide but a savior. While the *shravaka* aspires to the state of *arhat* (sanctity) the *bodhisattva* experiences ten stages in the service of his brothers and thus postpones reaching his *nirvana*. In the eyes of lay people, this personage becomes a subject worthy of admiration and devotion because he puts the salvation of others before all else. Moreover, a new doctrine in Buddhism developed, inspired by the inherent character of Buddhahood, the deep dimension of all things. Con-

1. A scene showing life in a village in the first period of the great diffusion of Buddhism in India under the Maurya, around 250 B.C. In the background there is a stupa, one of the most impressive architectural features of the ancient world. These are hemispherical constructions containing the relics of the Buddha or of important persons, or objects that belonged to the Buddha. The stupa can also be considered as the symbol of Buddhist law.
2. The third stupa at Sanci in India. In this most famous stupa, one can observe a harmika (belvedere) at the top, which also has a parasol, the

1 2

symbol of kingship. A balustrade at middle height makes it possible for the faithful to walk round in procession as a rite of worship (circumambulation). At that time the Buddha was not represented in human figure and the stupa itself represented the nirvana of the Buddha. As a result the stupas became true and proper sanctuaries, that is places of pilgrimage and cultic ritual.

trary to what the monks teach, it is believed that every individual participates the essence of the Buddha in the intimacy of his own being, thus opening his way toward the supreme Awakening. In this respect people refer to the *Mahayana* (or Large Vehicle), which carries a great number of beings to salvation.

In this transformation, that which had been the law of *karman* yields to the possibility that the merits obtained by the *bodhisattva* are transferred to the faithful, thereby allowing a belief in prayer and cult. Thus, together with the Buddhism of meditation, a Buddhism of faith was born. These two coexist to the present day.

5. On the great raised platform of the Buddhist complex of Borobudur in Java in Indonesia, hollow stupas were built, which contained statues of meditating Buddhas.
6. A bodhisattva in the temple of Candi Sari in Java in Indonesia.

3

4

3. A bodhisattva at the great rupestral sanctuary of Maijishan in China, 6th century.
4. A bodhisattva, an example of Gandhara art of India of the 3rd century.

5

6

BUDDHISM IN CHINA

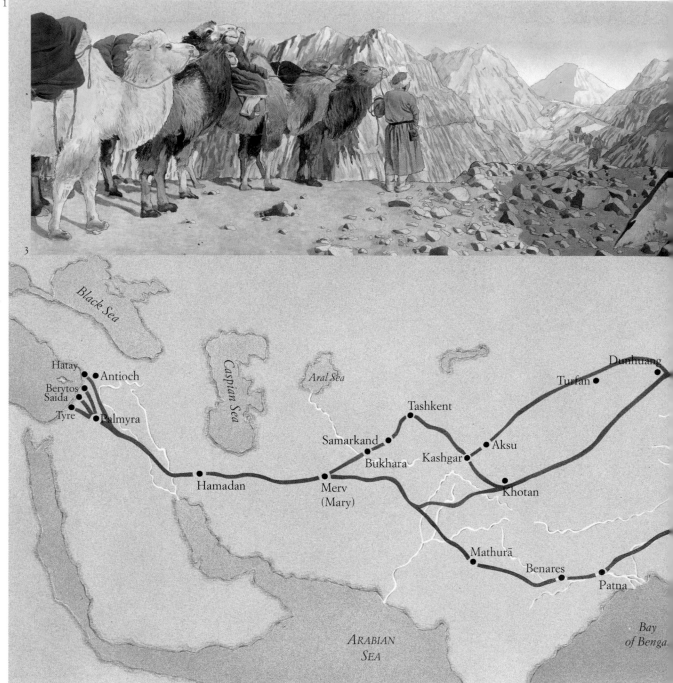

2. A Chinese monk at the end of the 7th century. He is carrying Buddhist scripts, after a long voyage, to his country.

Buddhist missionaries made their way to China during the first century A.D. along the Silk Route, preaching to both common men and to learned Taoists (adepts of Tao – 'the way' – which is central to one of the main philosophic and religious expressions of China). Listening to them, these Taoists felt that the missionaries were preaching a religion with the Buddha as its powerful god. This misunderstanding resulted in the first success of the Buddhism of the Small Vehicle in China.

The fall of the Han dynasty in 220 A.D. was followed by a period of instability, which opened the way to *Mahayana* missionaries who favored voyages and pilgrimages to India and Ceylon. These links gave birth to an original Chinese Buddhism, which included aspects of both Hindu doctrines and Taoist teachings, and led to the formation of two Buddhist schools.

Ch'an (which became Zen in Japan) is the Chinese form of the Buddhism of meditation. Drawing upon the Large Vehicle and on Tao, the masters Tao Cheng (360-434) and Sang Chao (384-414) taught that the nature of Buddha is a hidden treasure to be sought in every living being. In accordance with this belief, reading Buddhist texts or performing acts of piety is not required, but rather one must stop the work of the spirit to allow the inner light that will bring about the Enlightenment to flow. During the great persecution carried out by Emperor Wu-tsung in 845, devotees of Ch'an were forced to lay low, but the belief was revived and strengthened after the storm of persecution ended.

One of the great Buddhas of the Mahayana (emanations of an originary celestial Buddha, of whom Gautama, the historic

4

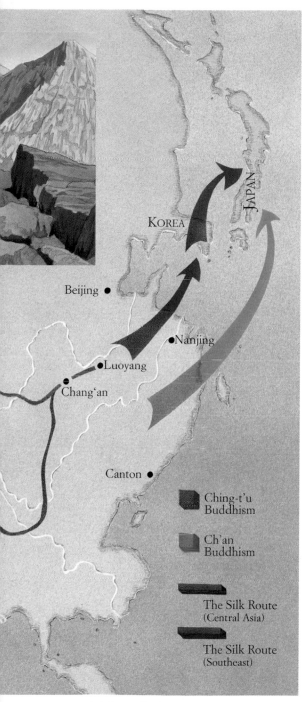

Buddha, is a manifestation) known as Amitabha was already known in China in the second century. Ching-t'u, the school known as that of the Pure Land or of the Western Paradise, began and developed devotion toward this Buddha, who was considered as sovereign in paradise. The contacts of this form of mystic Buddhism with Christianity and the Indian devotion of the *bhakti*, addressing gods close to man, led its disciples to practice the cult of Amitabha. This belief system emphasized the importance of living a high moral life, including adoration of statues, permanent thanksgiving, a religion of love, and a tranquil happiness that prepared the way to paradise after death. This form of Buddhism soon migrated to Korea, Japan, and Vietnam.

4. The sculptured grottoes of Dazú in Sichuan in China are an expression of Ching-t'u Buddhism.
5. Guangxiao Temple in China is the expression of Ch'an Buddhism. There the 6th-century monk Bodhidharma came to be considered as the patriarch of Ch'an Buddhism.

5

1. The Silk Route served to spread Buddhism, which from India passed through Afghanistan to reach China in the first century A.D., when direct contacts with India began. Ch'an Buddhism passed directly from China to Japan, becoming Zen, while Ching-t'u Buddhism passed to Korea and from there to Japan.
3. The journey from the Mediterranean to China was a long and difficult one, over 7,000 km long. Horses had to be exchanged for camels and Asian guides had to be used to lead travelers through the difficult passes.

8
TIBETAN BUDDHISM AND LAMAISM

1. Tibetan monks on the roof of the 9th-century monastery at Likir in the Himalayas.
2. The gompa or monastery at Thiksey in Ladakh, which dates back to the 15th century, is a typical example of a Himalayan monastery.
3. An nga, the typical ritual drum of Tibetan monks.

Tibet, 'the roof of the world,' with its great spaces and profound silence, was found to encourage religious thought. The pre-Buddhist religion, known as Bon, consisted of a complex of practices concerning the spirits (shamanism), nature cults, and magical rites, which may appear cruel to modern Westerners. In 779, the monk Padmasambhava came from the Kashmir and founded the great monastery of Bsam-yas, where many Buddhists gathered from various places to translate their Sanskrit texts into Tibetan. It was the foundation of the Buddhist sect known as the 'old believers' or 'red hats,' who were later dispersed during a persecution between 803 and 842.

In 1042 A.D., a second period of development was started when the monk Atisha reached Tibet from his native Bengal. Together with other monks from India and Kashmir, he founded many monasteries and re-organized monastic life to include a monastic hierarchy, with the lamas or religious leaders as its aristocracy. This Buddhism of the Large Vehicle included both married and celibate monks.

The monk Tsong Khapa, born in 1357 in eastern Tibet, introduced yet another reform. Returning to the Buddhism of Shakyamuni, he made his monks wear yellow tunics and hats. He dictated their daily activities and insisted upon celibacy, the practice of confession, fasting on prescribed days, and festivals. In 1578 a new title was conferred to the religious and political leader of Tibet — Dalai Lama, 'ocean teacher.' A monk, he was considered a reincarnation of Avalokitesh-

vara, a heavenly *bodhisattva* who has refused *nirvana* in order to look after humans with particular care and attention. Placed at the height of the social scale, the lamas are revered religious masters who enjoy great privileges. All intellectual life is concentrated in the monasteries — holy places where the cult is celebrated in a rather rich liturgical framework featuring an extraordinary variety of rites. Tibetans also use divination and oracles to explain events in their lives.

Since 1949, Chinese communists have invaded Tibet, imprisoning and executing thousands of monks and forcing many other thousands to marry. Of 3,700 great monasteries, which used to house more than 200,000 monks, more than 3,650 have been destroyed. Only a few hundred Tibetan monks remain. Much of the cultural wealth of the country has been annihilated, causing an irreparable damage to the heritage of mankind.

6

5

4. *Cham or ritual dances, which are veritable performances, are a feature of Tibetan Buddhism. The illustration shows the popular character of Padmasambhava who, as an Indian yogi, introduced Buddhism to Tibet in the 8th century. The dance is taking place in the monastery at Kampagar in northern India, where many Tibetan refugees have found shelter.*
5. *The Dalai Lama taking part in a ceremony in the monastery at Namgyal in northern India. He is holding a dordje in his hands, the symbol of Tibetan Buddhism.*
6. *A center of studies for Tibetan Buddhism in Bourgogne in France.*

9

BUDDHISM IN JAPAN

Chinese Buddhism arrived in Japan by way of Korea 1,000 years after its founding. There it encountered the Shinto, 'the way of the gods,' a Neolithic religion built on the presence of *kami*, powerful supernatural beings. The Emperor Shotoku Taishi (574-622) built the first monasteries and embraced the new religion, which gave the country a new moral structure and a world vision, although restricted to the ruling class. In

being organized at Kamakura, where a great number of monasteries were located. Zen proclaimed Awakening without preparation. Its main protagonist was the monk Dogen (1200-1253) who believed that Buddhahood was an innate feature of human nature to which one must only awaken. Through the practice of Zazen, 'sitting meditation,' the disciple achieves Awakening. Each disciple must liberate his spirit

1

the eighth century, there developed an original form of Japanese Buddhism called Ryobushinto, which was an amalgam of Shinto and Buddhism, the encounter between the *kami* and the *bodhisattva*. In an attempt to achieve an equilibrium between these 'two halves of a cloven piece of wood' and thus encourage national unity, the authorities embraced this new religion. In this preoccupation to adapt to the needs of particular epochs, however, schools and sects proliferated, centering around the two areas of devotion and meditation.

The Buddhism of devotion searched for its way at first in chanting, in prayer, and in ecstasy, and later in the doctrine of Jodo (Pure Land). An outstanding figure of Jodo, the monk Honen (1133-1212) taught the Nembutsu, a practice of simply calling upon the name of Buddha, constantly and with deep devotion, to obtain salvation. The Nembutsu led the believers to achieve the Buddhahood. Honen's disciple, the monk Shinran (1173-1262), broke the law of celibacy for monks and denounced study as a means to achieve wisdom, steering Buddhism in the direction of a popular monotheism.

While the Buddhism of faith as preached by Honen and Shinran was diffusing, Zen (a Buddhism of meditation) was

1. Shinto shrine at Izumo, in Japan. Shinto, the traditional religion of Japan, is linked to the cult of natural forces. When Buddhism arrived in Japan, it was influenced by Shinto.
2. The famous Buddhist sanctuary of Horyuji at Nara in Japan. Nara was the old capital which welcomed Buddhism as a new religion. On the left there is the very high pagoda with the relics, while on the right there is the kondo, the principal building used for ceremonies. The plan of the monastery can be seen in the top left-hand corner.

from every tie and overcome all mental agitation to achieve *satori*, an illumination which is an intuitive vision. Zen has been applied to the art of war, the tea ceremony, the art of gardening, and to painting.

Nembutsu and Zen fit Japanese culture perfectly and today constitute two important branches of modern Buddhism, with Zen also being well received in the West.

3. *Amitabha, known as Amida in Japan. Painting of the Japanese Kamakura period (1200-1300).*

4. Zen garden in Kyoto in Japan. It is a garden of rocks and sand which have been raked for centuries with the same movements.

5. *A house for the tea ceremony in a park near Tokyo in Japan.*
6. *The Eaton Commercial Center in Toronto in Canada. This is a symbol of the contemporary world, exhausted by consumption and goods. Buddhism enters it to propose a form of peace.*

10
THE *BODHISATTVA,* SAVIOR AND SAVED

THE VOW OF THE *BODHISATTVA*

May I be the protector of the abandoned, the guide of those who walk and, for those who aspire to reach the other bank, the boat, the dam, the bridge; may I be the lamp for those who need a lamp, the bed for those who need a bed, the slave for those who need a slave ... Just as the earth and the other elements serve the multiple uses of the innumerable beings scattered in infinite space, so may I be useful in any possible way to the beings who inhabit this space, until everyone is liberated.

Śantideva, *The Way to Light,* III

This text clearly summarizes the vow and the ideal of the *bodhisattva,* a savior created by the *Mahayana* Buddhists at the beginning of our era, standing in contrast to the *arhat* of the *Hinayana* Buddhists of the preceding five centuries. Achieving the highest level of Buddhist compassion, which he transforms into an aspiration for universal Awakening, the *bodhisattva* renounces his own immediate definitive liberation through the Awakening to look after other beings.

Such a profound compassion makes him a "saved savior" who penetrates the hearts, responds to the various spiritual needs of all creatures, and who reaches down to the human caravan to carry its burden of suffering. This path starts with a vow, which lies at the origin of the numerous merits that the *bodhisattva* will accumulate, a reserve made available to the other creatures and from which they can draw, through their devotion toward these saviors. The first among them is Avalokiteshvara, 'a great ocean of virtues worthy of every homage.'

Thus, in parallel with the Buddhism of meditation, there developed a Buddhism of devotion with a cult of saviors.

1. *A sculpture showing a standing Buddha making a welcoming gesture towards the sufferings of mankind. This sculpture is located at the entrance to one of the rupestral temples at Ajanta in India.*
2. *Chittagong in Bangladesh. The tragedy of a starving population asking for help following the destruction caused by a cyclone in April 1991.*
3. *A detail of a tanka, a Tibetan painting on cloth from the 17th-18th century, showing the bodhisattva Avalokiteshvara. The position and the expression both transmit a sense of calm and peace.*

27

GLOSSARY

In this glossary there are only about 30 Sanskrit terms
which are useful to understand the text.
Words in CAPITALS are cross references

Amitabha Known in Japan as **Amida**, he is a BUDDHA, serving as a symbol of the purity of the soul and of spiritual Awakening, a representative of life after death, and as such fervently venerated in China, in Japan, and in South East Asia. Amitabha is especially revered in pietist monasteries, whose monks stress the need for a devout life nourished by religious sentiments. An entire literature about paradise or Amitabha's land of domicile has developed within this Buddhism of devotion (**amidism**).

Ananda 'beatitude.' The name of one of the BUDDHA's cousins, his disciple and the guide of the community after his death. As 'the first listener to the word,' he played a fundamental role in the council of Rajagrha and has been credited with the compilation of the first Buddhist SUTRA.

anatman 'absence of the self.' This is the way Buddhism expresses the doctrine of the non-existence of a personality, of a 'self.' The individual exists as a complex of psychic phenomena but not as a personal being.

arhat 'worthy, saintly, respectable.' Epithet of the BUDDHA, but also of the saint who has completed the Path of Liberation in this life, and has therefore reached NIRVANA, and will not be re-born again.

aryasatya 'noble truth.' **Catvary aryasatyani** The four noble truths about suffering, the origin of suffering, the surcease of suffering, on the path that leads to the end of suffering, as they were preached by the BUDDHA in his sermon in Benares.

Ashoka Third emperor (272-236 B.C.) of the Maurya dynasty of Magadha. A convert to Buddhism and founder of a great empire, Ashoka was tolerant and preoccupied with the well-being of his subjects. He wrote numerous edicts that were sculpted in the rock and on columns to make of the Buddhist DHARMA the basis of human and social ethics.

bhagavan or **bhagavat** 'blessed.' One of the epithets of the BUDDHA.

bhikshu A Buddhist monk, a bonzo; **bhikshuni** Buddhist nun.

bodhi (from *budh* 'to awaken'). The awakening of the supreme consciousness that allows one to see within oneself the sequence of all one's previous existences and to recognize the cause of suffering and rebirth. Thanks to the *bodhi*, the BUDDHA discovered the concatenation of cause and effect that liberated him from the cycle of rebirth.

bodhisattva An awakened man who has renounced Buddha-

hood to help others achieve the BODHI. This renunciation our of pure compassion is a doctrine that began five centuries after the beginning of Buddhism. It has become one of the pillars of religious Buddhism.

Buddha The Awakened One who has discovered the true knowledge and consciousness of the real state of all creatures and things by means of the opening of his mind. Siddhartha Gautama, also called Shakyamuni, 'the Sage of the Shakya,' was the first Awakened One. He discovered the four sacred truths and has therefore become a guide for all humanity. In the course of time, Buddhism turned to other Buddhas, in addition to the historic one, who were figures of the essence of Buddha.

cakra 'wheel.' A Sanskrit word, an Indian symbol of fullness, which in Buddhism symbolizes the fullness of the law (DHARMA), but also the cycle of rebirth and the impermanence of creatures and of things – i.e., their essentially transitory character – since the wheel touches the ground only for a brief moment as it moves forward.

Dharma 'the law.' The Buddhist doctrine, one of the Three Jewels of Buddhism, together with the BUDDHA and the community (SAMGHA). These three treasures constitute three 'refuges.' The Dharma consists of the laws to which all living beings and things, all phenomena, and all ideas must submit.

dhatu 'foundation.' That which is placed or established. They are the elements of sensory consciousness, i.e., those of the six organs, of the six objects, and of the six corresponding awarenesses. They are also the material elements: earth, water, fire, and wind. They are also the three worlds of desire (**kama**), of the forms (**rupa**), and of the non-forms (**arupya**).

duhkha 'suffering.' A Buddhist concept of suffering that constitutes the first of the four noble truths. It is the lot of all beings who are tied to the cycle of rebirth (SAMSARA). It is evil in the form of corporal and mental pain, evil in the form of oppression, and evil that derives from impermanence.

jnana Transcendent knowledge and awareness of the ultimate Reality. In Buddhism it is the knowledge about the holy truths, beings, and objects, as well as the overcoming of passion.

karman The 'law of actions,' which says that each action produces its effects on the cumulative spiritual totality of each living being and on his or her cosmic future. Each action possesses in itself a moral value, which can be good, bad, or neutral.

lama Buddhist religious of Tibet, Nepal, Sikkim, and Bhutan. The title is theoretically reserved to the superiors of monasteries, but is actually given to all monks. The Dalai Lama is the supreme head of Lamaism, who until 1950 lived in Lhasa in Tibet.

marga 'path,' **astangamarga**, 'eight paths of perfection.' This is the fourth truth of Buddhism, the eightfold path by means of which the disciple reaches NIRVANA. Buddhism is a middle way that preconizes morality and wisdom by keeping a balance between an ascetic rigor and an ecstatic mysticism.

nirvana 'extinction.' The point of non-return of the SAMSARA, liberation from the cycle of rebirth with the achieving of absolute beatitude, perfect happiness, an unalterable joy. The **parinirvana** is the complete extinction that takes place with the death of an ARHAT or a BUDDHA who has reached the fullness of happiness.

prajna Wisdom, intelligence, faculty of understanding and comprehending.

samadhi A stable position of the psychic being obtained through a severe discipline and a mental concentration, which leads to the complete unification of thought on one chosen subject. In Japanese Zen, one can reach the *samadhi* without a preparation following a psychic or psychological trauma.

Samgha The community of Buddhist religious; one of the three 'jewels' of the faithful together with the BUDDHA and the DHARMA.

samsara The cycle of rebirth that conditions the lives of living beings according to their KARMAN or retribution of actions. The only way of breaking out of this cycle is to achieve NIRVANA.

Śantideva A Buddhist philosopher of the seventh century who came from Saurastra in India. He wrote a religious epic poem, a collection of teachings, and a collection of SUTRAS.

satya 'reality, truth.' In particular, the four holy truths of suffering, the origin of suffering, the surcease of suffering, and of the path that leads to the end of suffering.

skandha 'aggregate.' Any of the five groups of phenomena which together make up the 'person.'

stupa Buddhist monument originating from the funerary tumulus. It consists of a tower, generally in the shape of a bell, where the relics of the historic BUDDHA, a saint, or of one who has reached Buddhahood are kept.

sutra 'thread.' A story which contains a sermon by the BUDDHA or one of his disciples.

Sutrapitaka 'basket of SUTRA.' A part of the ancient Buddhist canon containing the sermons and texts connected with it.

Tao, Taoism One of the most ancient versions of the genesis of man and his place in the universe, in addition to one of the most refined forms of natural spirituality of humankind. Its principal text is the *Tao Te King* (The Book of the Way and of Virtue), a collection of aphorisms and poems which can be defined as a brief treatise of natural mysticism.

Vinayapitaka 'basket of discipline.' A part of the Buddhist canon containing the precepts regarding monastic organization, life, and discipline.

Index